EMN

the wa

LEADERS' RESOURCES

EMMAUS
the way of faith

LEADERS' RESOURCES

Leading an Emmaus group

Stephen Cottrell, Steven Croft,
John Finney, Felicity Lawson and Robert Warren

Illustrations by Clare Parker

Second edition

Church House Publishing
Church House
Great Smith Street
London SW1P 3AZ

ISBN 978 0 7151 4472 5

Second edition published 2004
by Church House Publishing

First published 1998 by The National Society/Church House Publishing and Bible Society

Copyright © Stephen Cottrell, Steven Croft, John Finney, Felicity Lawson and Robert Warren 1998, 2002, 2004

Illustrations copyright © Clare Parker 2004

The right of Stephen Cottrell, Steven Croft, John Finney, Felicity Lawson and Robert Warren to be identified as the authors of this work has been asserted in accordance with the Copyright, Design and Patents Act 1988.

All rights reserved. No part of this publication may be reproduced or stored or transmitted by any means or in any form, electronic or mechanical, including photocopying, recording, or any information storage and retrieval system without written permission which should be sought from the Copyright Administrator, Church House Publishing, Church House, Church House, Great Smith Street, London SW1P 3AZ
email copyright@churchofengland.org

Acknowledgement

The Scripture quotations contained herein are from *The New Revised Standard Version of the Bible* copyright © 1989 by the Division of Christian Education of the National Council of the Churches of Christ in the USA.
All rights reserved.

Cover design by Church House Publishing

Printed in England by Ashford Colour Press, Gosport, Hampshire

Contents

Introduction		vii
1	Scriptural leadership	1
	Principle One	1
	Principle Two	2
2	Jesus the adult education expert	6
	Training	10
3	Emmaus leadership	11
	How many leaders do you need?	11
4	Getting going	13
	How often do we meet?	15
	Where do we meet?	18
	How do we arrange the venue?	19
	Preparing to lead a session	20
5	Growth groups	22
	Praise and Prayer	23
	Sharing	24
	Action	24
	Learning	25
	Ministry	27

6	Meals and ministry	28
	To eat or not to eat?	28
	Meals	29
	Going away	31

Epilogue 33
Bibliography on teaching adults 35
The authors 36

Introduction

Are you leading or going to lead an *Emmaus* course? If so you will already have realized that you have much to learn. At least, I hope so, because if not, you ought not to be responsible for a group at all. Leaders who are not also learners (the meaning of 'disciple' in the Bible) are a menace.

Group leadership is a skill we never entirely master. A group can always surprise us and there are always new things we can learn to make sure that we are communicating good news. Whether you have never led a group before or have done it scores of times, there are always things to find out.

Leading an *Emmaus* group needs

> organization
>
> care for people
>
> prayer – solid, persistent, faithful
>
> common sense
>
> an adaptable sense of humour –
> don't get too grim about it
>
> some knowledge.

Read this booklet before you begin. It is better to learn before you begin rather than discover your mistakes after you have led a group.

This booklet comes in two parts. The first two chapters deal with the *attitude* that leaders should have towards their group – learning from the Bible how we should regard those for whom God has given us responsibility. The rest of the book deals with the practicalities of leading a group.

If there is to be more than one leader (which is best), read this booklet through together before you begin.

Each of the different *Emmaus* books has an introduction which gives an outline of how leaders should tackle the sessions in the book: read this before using the material.

What is *Emmaus*?

Emmaus is divided into two unequal parts:

1. the fifteen-session Nurture book;
2. the pick 'n' mix Growth material in four books.

Alongside these there are three booklets:

- *Introduction;*
- *Contact;*
- *Leading an Emmaus Group.*

There is also *Youth Emmaus* for those between 11 and 16, and a series of *Emmaus* Bible Resources for those who want to dig deeper into the Bible.

(For a complete list of the main *Emmaus* material see the end of this booklet.)

This booklet deals with leading both Nurture and Growth groups. There are many differences and it is important to recognize which part is being referred to.

However, while *Emmaus* was initially designed to be used to help a group of people to faith through the Nurture course and then build them up through the Growth material, it is now being used in many other ways:

- as teaching material for existing house groups;
- for a whole congregation as teaching during a sermon (photocopying the appropriate pages for everyone);
- as a Lent course for groups or a mid-week service (choosing an appropriate four or five sessions from one of the *Emmaus* books);
- one-to-one – either when a more mature Christian helps another along the way, or when an excited group member tells a friend or relation what they have just learnt;
- as material for groups of churches studying together;
- as base material for school RE lessons.

Scriptural leadership

chapter 01

The two main principles of group leadership are in the Bible:

Principle One

'Whoever wants to be first must be last of all and servant of all' (Mark 9.35). If you are to lead an *Emmaus* group (or anything else for that matter) you are to be a servant of the people in the group.

Just think what this means:

- the people in the group are more important than you are (after all if they were not there you would not have a group in the first place!);
- what you teach is less important than what they learn (remember those hot summer afternoons at school when you learnt nothing at all despite all the teaching that was going on?);
- your job is to serve them (pray for and love them in the Name of Jesus).

What matters is our *attitude*. If we care for people, respect them, genuinely seek their good, put their interests first, then we shall be good leaders. If we want our views to prevail, meetings to be at our convenience and others to do what we want, we break the first scriptural principle.

If you want to do a Bible Study on Principle One, look at Luke 17.7-10; Colossians 3.23,24; Matthew 25.14-30; Philippians 2.3-11; Mark 10.42-45; John 15.12-17.

To sum up:

Leadership should be an expression of love

This should be your attitude when:

- You are preparing a session (and you haven't much time);
- You are teaching (and noticing how people are reacting);
- People ask for your time and energy (when you are feeling tired);
- People need to grow from under your care to take responsibility for themselves (when you are really wanting them to go on being dependent on you);
- You are praying for them (and many other things try to crowd them out).

Principle Two

Jesus 'when he saw the crowds, he had compassion for them, because they were harassed and helpless, like sheep without a shepherd.' (Matthew 9.36)

'Look at all the lonely people' – the Beatles song makes us ask questions.

This principle stems from the first. If we are concerned for people we have to look carefully at who they are, what background they have, what they do or do not know, and so on. The practical questions that arise, particularly before people come on the Nurture course, are:

Where have they come from?

Some people in the group will have a great deal of experience of the Christian faith and of the life of the Church: they know its language, its ways of doing things.

Others may not know one end of the Bible from the other, don't know the Lord's prayer, have hardly been inside a church, don't know even the simplest facts about the life of Jesus.

A leader who assumes that everyone in the group knows the same and has had the same experience is ignoring Principle Two and letting down the group.

Use the gifts of the group members: get the experienced ones to explain the in-language of the Church and encourage simple questions from the inexperienced.

'Blessed is the group which has a member who is so simple-hearted that they ask the questions everyone is dying to ask but dare not.'

Adults are frightened of appearing silly. People enrol on Cordon Bleu cookery courses and will try to conceal their ignorance of how many grams there are in a kilo.

'For months before the course started I used to dream about looking stupid… I was astonished at myself – a Cambridge First and worried about going back to school.' People on the course may never have read anything seriously or have been faced with visual aids, take-home leaflets and all the other bits of paper. They will need help to study in this way, and all the encouragement in the world.

Why are they here?

Some will come because they know they have spiritual needs:

Jane has been in the church for years and just wants a 'wash and brush up' of her faith.

John senses that despite all the years he has sung in the choir he has missed something vital.

Jennifer has come with a friend and knows next to nothing but is intensely curious.

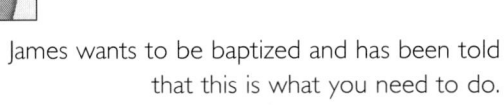

James wants to be baptized and has been told that this is what you need to do.

Jemima has a deep spiritual hunger and has read a lot of New Age material but knows hardly anything about the Christian faith: she is still searching.

Others will come for all sorts of very ordinary reasons:

William has come because he is fond of Jennifer and wants to be with her.

Winifred has just been through a divorce and needs company.

Wilfred is a combative sort of person and just likes a good argument.

There are a myriad different reasons why people come, and as leader it is important that you know what they are looking for.

Remember that we seldom have just one motive for doing things – spiritual and practical and all-too-human are mixed up. So don't be alarmed if someone who appears really to want to know Jesus also says 'The darts team has folded up and I wanted something to do on a Thursday evening.'

People in a **Nurture** group can usually be put in one of five categories:

1. *Cradle Christians* – who have been in the Church for a long time and who want a refresher course, or are beginning to think that there must be more to the Christian faith than turning up for an hour on a Sunday morning.
2. *Transfers* – those who have recently joined the Church from another congregation and who want to find out what makes it tick.
3. *Young Christians* – who are hungry to find out more and more about the faith.

4   *Enquirers* – those who want to find out about the Christian faith:
   a) some of these will have already decided that they want to become Christians – usually they ask for baptism or confirmation;
   b) others will be much less certain – they simply want to find out what the Christian faith is all about. They have no idea about deeper commitment at this stage.
5   *Returnees* – those who have drifted away from the Church long ago and have come back for another look.

Those who are very uncertain may need to start with their own agenda – which is themselves. Putting them straight into the Nurture course, which plunges them immediately into the being of God, could be too sudden. For them the five sessions on Personal Identity (Growth book *Christian Lifestyle*) may be the right place to begin as a short introductory course before they begin the Nurture course. Others want to know about prayer and the four sessions on the Lord's Prayer (Growth book *Growing as a Christian*) would be suitable. Both have also been found useful for church people who are not used to meeting in groups.

People in a **Growth** group will have different reasons for being there:

1   *Emmaus veterans* – they have been through the Nurture stage, enjoyed it and want to find out more.
2   *House groupies* – those who are used to house groups with their mixture of Bible teaching, discussion and prayer.
3   *Newcomers* – those who have just joined and to whom being in a group is very strange. They may or may not have some basic Christian knowledge.

As you look at the people who are going to make up your group you will recognize that they are unique. And the next group you meet with will also be unique. You may think that this means you should adjust the course to suit the needs of each particular group. Excellent: this is exactly how the *Emmaus* course should be used.

Jesus the adult education expert

chapter 02

Jesus knew how to communicate so that the 'crowds heard him gladly'. We ought humbly to come and see how he did it:

Jesus prayed

He was in constant touch with his Father. Pray by yourself and with the other leaders for every group member, and the families and contexts they come from. Pray also for yourself that you may care for, help and encourage them. It was after the disciples had seen Jesus praying by himself that they came and asked, 'Lord, teach us to pray' (Luke 11.1,2).

Jesus listened

People poured out their troubles to him and he patiently heard them out before he spoke. Good leadership means listening – really listening – to everybody in the group. Talkative or reserved, they need their say.

---

1. I listen least when I am most anxious to speak.

    Leaders – keep your eyes open for someone who wants to get a word in.

2. I stop listening when I think I know what the other person is going to say.

    Leaders – gently stop people from repeating themselves – and don't repeat yourself!

3. I evaluate what is said by my feelings about the speaker.

    Leaders – awkward people often ask good questions; help their contributions to be valued.

4. If my emotions are running high it is difficult to hear what another person is saying.

    Leaders – calm the group and start the discussion again (possibly with you making the points which caused conflict).

Leaders should remember that people do not listen to them if:
- they ramble on.
- they make too many points at once.
- they are aggressive.
- they exaggerate.
- their body language indicates that they are not interested in what others are saying.

(from research by Brian Cranwell)

Jesus was not afraid to teach

Sometimes today people are so encouraged to 'share their experience' that they never hear the Christian faith presented in a way which is captivating and coherent. In the Sermon on the Mount and elsewhere Jesus gave an awe-inspiring account of Christian belief and practice.

But note:

- Jesus was not afraid to keep some things hidden. He did not put the whole banquet on one plate.

- He wanted people to think for themselves so he did not give pat answers – the best answers provoke more questions. He set up guideposts but expected people to work out the details of the route for themselves: look at the Sermon on the Mount. Give people space to work things out.

- He was straight with people. He did not pretend that following him was going to be roses, roses all the way – nor did he make it seem so drear that nobody in their right mind would want to become a disciple. Today people don't believe hype and spin – they are super-saturated with adverts. And we should not 'sell' the gospel or make it so life-denying that the joy of Christ does not shine through.

- He was passionate about his message. Leaders need to be so soaked in Christian truth that they are thrilled to the core.

Jesus did not mind being interrupted

In John 14 he listened carefully to Thomas and Philip as they blurted out questions and then gave them a full answer. Research shows that people listen far more carefully to the answers to questions than they do to straight teaching. The *Emmaus* course expects leaders to be flexible enough to adapt to the needs of the group, to answer people's real questions. The agenda of the people in the group is more important than what is in the notes – or our pet hobby-horse.

Jesus showed what he taught

He did not just talk about love – he showed them love.

He did not just talk about healing – he laid hands on people.

He did not just talk about prayer – he was in constant contact with the Father.

He did not just talk about vulnerability – he went to the cross.

Paul could say, 'our message of the gospel came to you not in word only, but also in power and in the Holy Spirit and with full conviction' (1 Thessalonians 1.5). It may make us uncomfortable but we have to face the truth that many newcomers in the group will see us as showing them what a Christian should be like.

Jesus told stories

Some of us find it easy to talk in abstractions, especially if we think we know some theology. We need to remember that the atonement began with the story of a man being tortured to death, the incarnation is about a baby in a stable, the coming of the Spirit is about what happened to a group of people.

Most of Jesus' stories are about people – the tabloids know that stories about a 'petite, thirty-two-year-old, brunette shop assistant' catch people's attention. And most of the people he talked about were not celebrities: he talked about a fisherman, a small businessman, a father whose heart ached for his son, a housewife who had lost a coin and desperately turned the house upside down to find it.

Jesus referred to the Bible constantly, but he also looked around him and took in the contemporary world and spoke about ordinary people's worries and happinesses. And when he did so he told stories so that they could take it in.

There are three stages of learning:

> **Knowledge** – learning facts
>
> **Understanding** – getting hold of what those facts mean
>
> **Application** – making the facts your own

Think how this applies to the crucifixion: knowing the story…understanding its real meaning…bowing before the wonder of it in repentance and praise.

Good teachers start with knowledge (it can be too easily assumed that everyone knows the facts) and then go on to the others. Poor teachers start with understanding or even application.

'Most Christian leaders underestimate the intelligence of their congregation, and overestimate their knowledge.'

Jesus challenged people

He said to people 'follow me'; he told the rich man to 'sell all that you have'; he questioned the people who were so certain they were right. Most searchingly of all he said to Peter and to us, 'do you love me?'.

We should not hesitate, after a lot of prayer and thought, to ask people about their response to the good news they have heard. To fail to do this is to let them down; it leaves them with their noses pressed to the cake shop window without showing them the way in.

To lead an *Emmaus* course is an immense privilege because we are helping people at a very sensitive time in their lives – when they are finding Christ for themselves. The least we can give them is thorough preparation and a willingness to keep on learning the skills of leadership. And we can learn from the master Teacher who knew what was in the hearts of men and women and how to warm them with the fire of the gospel.

Training

There are two kinds of ways people can learn:

Apprentice	**Student**
(think of craftsman passing on his skill)	(think of undergraduate studying)
In the workplace near home	In college away from home
Through hands-on experience	Through books/lectures
Through repetition	Without repetition (you don't go to the same lecture twice)
Through personal contact with a teacher	Without much personal contact
It's slow (but what is learnt sticks)	It's fast (but what is learnt tends to be easily forgotten)
It's threatening (if you get it wrong your teacher is at your elbow)	It's emotionally cool
It's often done in a group	You're on your own (is there anything more lonely than an exam room?)
It's mainly practical	It's mainly theoretical

The best training is generally left hand with a bit of right hand, i.e. practice with explanation.

Which method did Jesus use to train his disciples????

Emmaus leadership

An *Emmaus* group is intended to bring people to God and build them up in their faith. Apart from worship, is there any more important work for God that you can do than help in this?

Running an *Emmaus* **Nurture** group is one of the most challenging and worthwhile things which any Christian can do. It s-t-r-e-t-c-h-e-s you because it demands so many different gifts. You need to have some of the gifts of:

- an **evangelist** to lead people to Christ – who **guides** to the Way;
- a **pastor** to help the vulnerable – who **helps** along the Way;
- a **teacher** who helps others to learn the faith – who **tells us** about the Way;
- an **administrator** to get it all organized – who **smooths** the Way.

This faces you with an immediate and very important question:

How many leaders do you need?

It is highly unlikely that one person will have all the gifts that a group needs – even if that person is a minister!

Therefore you may well need another leader beside yourself. Two or more leaders can bring:

- different personal gifts;
- variety in the teaching ministry;
- companionship and prayer support;
- someone to share the load with.

People in a group tend to identify with someone who is like themselves. Since the group you will be leading will probably have both men and women of different ages, it is ideal if your co-leaders can be of a different sex and age to yourself.

While it is not always possible to have more than one leader there is no doubt that this is best – and from now on this booklet assumes that Nurture group leadership is plural.

Notice that the gifts needed for leadership of a **Growth** group are rather different:

- there is less need for the gifts of an evangelist;
- pastoral gifts are still needed – though there may be fewer demands as members of the group learn to care for each other;
- teaching gifts are still very important but it is essential that the group should be allowed to explore for itself. 'Chalk and talk' teachers are lethal for such a group, for they do not allow members to grow;
- administrative gifts continue to be important because a group that does not know what is happening will founder.

Some of these gifts can be looked for among the members of the group itself:

- the administration can be delegated to other group members;
- group members can be encouraged to care for each other by visiting in sickness, giving practical help in crisis and praying at all times;
- some of the teaching can be done by group members.

In other words a Growth group is half way between a Nurture group and a house group. It is possible that only one leader may be sufficient (provided they can delegate).

Chapter 04
Getting going

Nurture courses often assume that you already have a group of people longing to join. In the average church this is seldom the case and so the *Emmaus Contact* booklet describes how to get a group together and how to introduce the course. You will certainly find it worthwhile to read this thoroughly – preferably going through it with potential *Emmaus* group leaders (Chapter 10 of *Contact* gives you a short course to do together).

Common faults when starting an *Emmaus* group are:

- Starting too hurriedly – or putting it off so that it never happens!
- Little prayer.
- No preparation of leaders.
- Failure to integrate it into the life of the church.
- Poor administration – no one knows what is happening.
- Over-ambition – starting with too many groups can lead to exhaustion.

Steps which need to be taken:

1. Look carefully through the *Emmaus* material and read together the Introduction. It is important that you feel comfortable with the flexible nature of the course and distinguish between the Nurture and the Growth elements.
2. It is introduced to, and owned by, the church – since the whole congregation is involved to a greater or lesser extent.
3. Prayer is made by all the church.
4. An introductory meeting is arranged (see *Contact* booklet Chapter 9).
5. The first sessions are arranged.
6. The first group is formed.

Note

- Don't wait until you have a group of people waiting before arranging an *Emmaus* course. Time and again it has been shown that the right way is to arrange for a group whether or not you know of people wanting to go on it. Then PRAY people onto the course. If you think it is right to begin a course, launch out in faith.

- It is usually found that the first people who come onto the *Emmaus* Nurture course are church members who want another look at their faith. Once they are enthusiastic they invite their friends to come – and are glad to act as sponsors to newcomers.

- It has been found that churches that have used Nurture courses before tend to think of *Emmaus* as 'just another course' and need help in getting the idea of the Growth material. It has been found useful to duplicate the diagram of the overall plan, which is in the *Introduction* booklet, page 3, or to use the material on the CD-ROM accompanying the Nurture course. It can also help if existing house groups use some of the Growth material to get the feel of it. If house group members feel comfortable with it they will be more likely to invite their non-Christian friends to the Nurture groups.

- Some Nurture courses require you to follow a set pattern. *Emmaus* is more flexible than that and requires leaders to adapt the elements to the needs of the people on the course, i.e. it requires more preparatory work. Be ready for this.

- Think before the Nurture group begins what is going to happen to the group afterwards. There are four possibilities:

    a) The group just finishes and no further support is given. This may be appropriate if the group is made up of existing church members. It is criminal for newcomers to be left to sink or swim without the close help of others; they have discovered Christ with others and they need their continued help.

    b) The group finishes and the members are asked to join different house groups. This can work, especially if several members of the group go together to a house group. However, a house group develops a strong life of its own and its agenda may well not be suitable for those who are new to the faith. However welcoming it is, existing members and newcomers can feel excluded.

c) If the church does not have house groups but some sort of central weekly meeting or service, group members should be encouraged to go and sponsors will have a particularly important role to play in ensuring that group members are made welcome.

d) The group continues as a group – probably using some of the *Emmaus* Growth material.

In practice, if the group is mainly made up of newcomers or those who are not members of an existing house group, it has been found that (d) is the best answer – though new leaders will probably be needed if the best leaders of the vital Nurture courses are not to become tied down in leading Growth groups.

How often do we meet?

Most education these days is made up of modules – each one comparatively short and with a definite end.

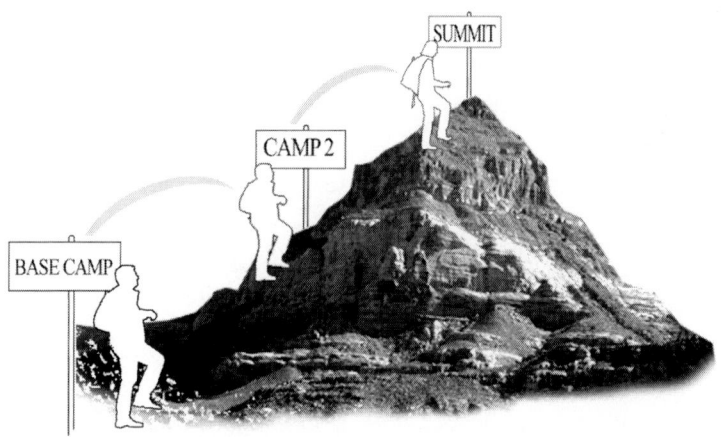

A long journey is best covered in short stages, particularly if people are uncertain. This is why the *Contact* booklet suggests a single introductory session to help people onto the course.

The idea of short stages does not stop there:

Emmaus **Nurture** material is intended to last for fifteen sessions, but it is divided into three sections. For people putting their big toe into the sea of the Christian faith a demand for a full fifteen sessions can be daunting. Some churches ask people to come to a fairly short set of sessions and then ask them if they want to go on to the next. Thus the fifteen-session Nurture course material has three sections of six, four and five sessions. These can be seen as intervals during a play or breaks during a journey.

But a Nurture course has a certain impetus to it. It should not be drawn out or interrupted too much. Some groups will want to do one section in weekly sessions, pause for a couple of weeks (during which there may be the appropriate services of welcome in church – see Nurture course pages 108–113), and then begin the next section. Other groups may want to do all fifteen sessions in as many weeks.

Things which need to be kept in mind are:

- The dynamics of the group – very quickly a group gets a life of its own and its members want to meet regularly. This is to be encouraged as much as possible for they are receiving much support from each other.
- Adults, especially the elderly, have considerable short-term memory loss. If sessions do not follow each other fairly quickly, much of a session can be taken in recalling what has already happened – frustrating for those who can remember!

The **Growth** material is also divided into sections of between three and five sessions.

There is a difference here between a Nurture group and a Growth group. The Nurture group follows a flexible pattern. A Growth group has choice – the members decide what subject it needs to learn about, how it is going to tackle this and how the group ought to run.

- A Nurture group has a set menu.
- A Growth group is à la carte.

Some of this is covered in the *Introduction* booklet, which is essential reading for leaders.

Agenda for first leaders' meeting:

1. Getting the group together – publicity and means of response
2. Who to ask personally
3. Arranging the introductory meeting
4. The congregation – how to involve them
5. Sponsors
6. Prayer
7. Services of welcome
8. Practical arrangements:
   a) Venue
   b) Arrangement of venue
   c) Frequency of meetings
   d) Dates for meetings
   e) Visual aids
   f) Ordering/photocopying of materials
   g) Music
   h) Refreshments/meals
   i) Weekend/retreats/quiet days
   j) Leaders' meetings – before, during and after the course.

Where do we meet?

Numbers often dictate the venue. If you have thirty or more people, you probably only have one or two places where you can meet – remembering that you will need to split such a large group from time to time into discussion groups, which will also need space.

If you have twelve or so people, they could meet in a living room – a squash is no bad thing certainly it is better than being huddled together in the corner of a 200-seater church hall.

Look at the people in your group again – would meeting on church premises put them off? Would meetings in one of their homes be a good thing – or would it mean that the host would always be fussing about the coffee? Is it right for one of the leaders to have it in their home – but what about the impact on the rest of the family, the stress of preparing each session, etc.? While most groups do meet in private homes it is good to think about the places that people in your community meet: it is good to be there, whether it is a pub, a community centre or a school.

One group met round a table in a room leading off the bar in a pub. Half way through the session they broke and went to get a drink. They came back with half a dozen friends who were intrigued as to what was going on. Soon the newcomers were joining in. One of them became a Christian that very evening as his wife said, 'he only asks questions when he has a couple of pints inside him'!

Would a very 'posh' home make some people feel uneasy?

Might a grubby home lead to some people making disparaging remarks?

An alternative is to go from house to house provided everybody has exact instructions as to how to get to each venue there may be advantages in this; **but** is there security for the members of the group (especially a Nurture group) in having the same venue?

WEEK 1   WEEK 2   WEEK 3

Avoid 'competitive catering' if going to different houses. This very practical question needs much thought and prayer. The wrong place can mean the group never gets going. Few churches have the perfect place, but if God has called you to start a group, the right place to hold it must exist.

How do we arrange the venue?

This is not as straightforward as might appear: think V A T S when looking at a possible venue:

V   **Visibility** – can everyone see everyone else?

It is difficult to have a discussion with people who are invisible. Therefore avoid rows. A common fault is to have chairs against a wall – X and Y cannot talk to each other without craning their heads forward.

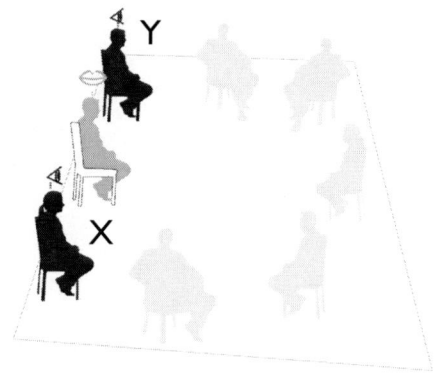

On the other hand, is the leader too visible – separate from the group like a teacher in a classroom? If so the idea of discovering the pathways of God together disappears.

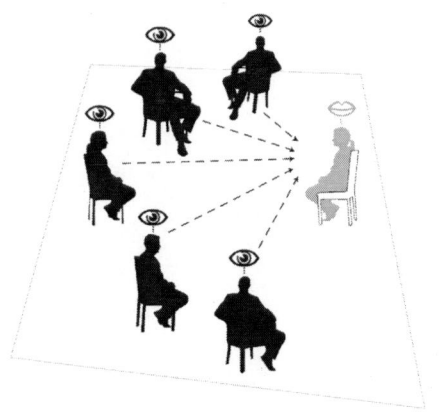

Getting going 19

A **Audibility** – can people hear each other? Remember that even in a smallish group it is likely that at least one person will have difficulty (about 10 per cent of people have impaired hearing). Being able to see the lips of the speaker is an important aid to them.

T **Temperature** – the usual difficulty in church halls is being too cold, with draughts whistling round people's feet. In people's homes it is usually the opposite – the host turns up the central heating, forgetting that twelve bodies in a room generate a good deal of heat themselves, so everyone becomes soporific and finds it hard to concentrate.

S **Seating** – are the seats like boards so that people are shifting uncomfortably in half an hour – or like beds so that they fall asleep? Often there is not much you can do about this – though getting people to move around is good practice see if you can put some movement into the session half-way through. (Research shows that adults learn best when there is a break every thirty to forty minutes).

Preparing to lead a session

For both **Nurture** and **Growth** groups:

Preparation is essential – it should be:

- prayerful and practical;
- thorough and flexible;
- in collaboration with other leaders.

A suggested pattern would be:

- Pray.
- Think about the last session:
  What did you learn from the members of the group?
  What went well in the teaching?
  What did not 'click'?
  Who did not come? Why?
  Does anyone need special help?
  Were the practical arrangements OK?

- Read through the material twice carefully. Get the aim of the session firmly in your mind.
- In the light of the people in your group, are there any parts which need to be stressed – or skipped over?
- Take each section in turn – what can you add to it:

    from the Bible?

    from your experience?
- Write notes on the teaching you are to give – and the approximate timing.

    (Some people like to write notes on the *Emmaus* book itself so that they are not referring to two pieces of paper.)
- Decide who is going to lead each part of the session.
- Think through the practical arrangements . . . VATS . . . food.
- Pray some more.

---

1. Teaching is best given in short periods so that people can discuss and think about each new thought. Leaders may have been going on if they speak without pause for more than four minutes.
2. As group members get to know each other they will want to talk more, so the amount of input by the leaders will decrease.
3. Remember the research which shows:

    'People remember best what they say themselves' – so the more leaders talk the less people learn!
4. A group session can last as long as a football match – ninety minutes with thirty minutes for extra time (if there is a knotty issue to be worked through or something that cannot wait until next time). However, sometimes it is fairer to people to say that each session is going to be over by a set time.
5. Visual aids generally need to be straightforward. 'It is important that the hypnotic effect of the more sophisticated media doesn't detract from the simpler and sometimes more effective visual aids' (Anton Baumohl, *Making Adult Disciples*).

Growth groups

chapter 05

Blobs

Look for and pray for 'blobs': those 'moments of insight' or the 'Eureka' moments when the penny drops and someone in your group has 'got it'.

Most people use 'blob' thinking most of the time, rather than linear:

A+B = C rational thinking.

Jesus used the telling phrase, the visual imagery and the parable to help 'blob' thinking – so should we.

'Play your holy hunches.'

    Archbishop Michael Ramsey

There should be five components to a **Growth** group – not every one should be present every time, but over a period all should be covered – P S A L M:

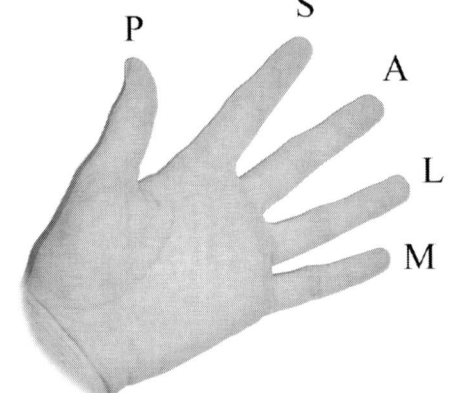

P	Praise and Prayer
S	Sharing
A	Action
L	Learning
M	Ministry

22 *Emmaus: Leading an Emmaus Group*

P   Praise and Prayer

In a Nurture group prayer is led mainly by the leaders. Virtually every Growth group session suggests a pattern for prayer and there is a need to develop the gifts of everyone in the group.

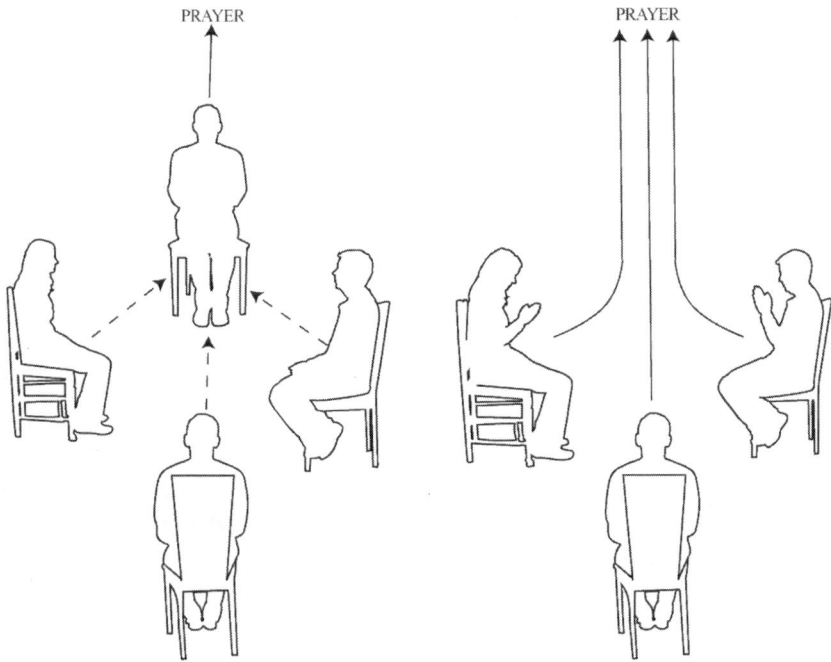

Prayer by other members of the group can be encouraged by:

- asking members to read a written prayer;
- suggesting that they think about people who are ill or in need;
- making the writing and reading out of a prayer part of the session;
- inviting short 'biddings' – please pray for…

Remember that many people find leading in prayer difficult and even embarrassing. Do not push people too far beyond the point when they feel comfortable.

As a Growth group matures, singing becomes more possible (provided that there are some musical skills available) and the group begins to develop its own repertoire. Do not suggest too many new songs or hymns – people often find the familiar is the best vehicle for worship.

S   Sharing

People should be helped to share their lives with each other. If we care for people we are interested in them:

- Encourage each other through our victories.
- Sympathize during the hard times.
- Offer practical help and counsel.

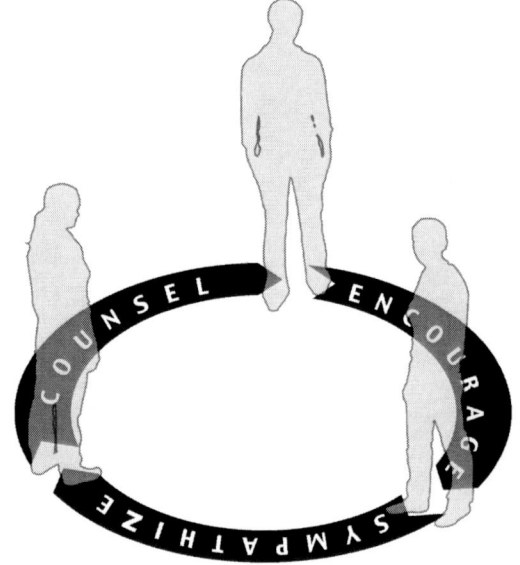

Note that

1 The group needs to be reminded from time to time of the importance of confidentiality.

2 Leaders need to step in if someone begins to share something which reveals too much of themselves – some personality types have a 'compulsion to tell', whether it is appropriate or not at the time.

3 Encourage the sharing of information. It is important to know that X's child is ill or that the future of Y's job is uncertain.

A   Action

A group without an outlet can become a stagnant pool. The outlet is action outside the group which puts into practice what has been learnt and experienced within it. It can be an individual doing something or the group as a whole carrying out a project. Some examples have been:

- Collecting for famine relief.
- Planting a new group.

- Painting a hall used by the community.
- Having a special time for prayer at a time of crisis.
- Giving money to help a group member move house.

The possibilities are endless.

L   Learning

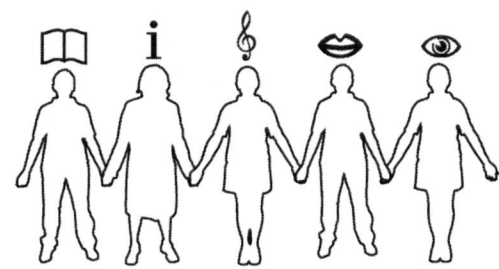

The section of *Emmaus* that the Growth group has chosen to study will be the focus of attention. As a group matures, the teaching should be increasingly shared with other members of the group:

- Someone can be asked to introduce a part of the session.
- Someone can be asked to make a visual aid, find an appropriate piece of music, act out a role.

It is good for a group occasionally to plan the next session together so that everyone can have a chance to say how they would tackle the subject.

'We put an enormous premium on mental speed – quickness of response and grasp. The slow thinker is lost and may never catch up. Yet it is our experience that, given time and an uncompetitive environment, the greatest advances, the most profound contribution, the real intellectual exercising comes as much from the slow ones as from the quick ones… it is the slow plodders grappling with new ideas until they master them, who get to the heart of the matter.'

Jennifer Rogers, *Adults Learning*, Open University Press

Is there any point in asking a question if no one can answer it? It just puts people down.

The Fine Art of Squelching

The ability to squelch the life out of an *Emmaus* group may be thought of as an art. Because of the strong interest in this new art, the following ground rules are offered to would-be squelchers who wish to develop their talents in this direction.

1 Dominate the group from the beginning. Establish yourself as the authority on all matters.

2 Keep the discussion on a theoretical plane. Mention names like Kierkegaard, Schleiermacher and Tillich occasionally to make the others feel inferior.

3 Deliver a learned lecture at each meeting. (Our rock-bound guarantee – the group won't last three months or your money back!)

4 **Pay no attention to the needs and interests of the group members**. Most people don't know what's best for them anyhow.

5 Don't let others lead the discussion; they might get too interested.

6 Never allow group members to share anything personal. Change the subject to a nice safe intellectual discussion when this happens.

7 Don't encourage every member to talk. Limit the discussion to the more vocal, intellectual members in order to maintain a high level of sophistication. If you urge the silent ones to speak they might think that their ideas count after all.

8 Allow one or two people to dominate the discussion. That way the others will become quietly angry and the group will fold up in no time.

9 Answer all questions yourself. Don't let group members speak to each other or answer each other's questions. What do they know that you can't say better?

10 Complain at every meeting how few have turned up. This will make those who have come size conscious and give them a sense of guilt.

Adapted from Clyde Reid, *Groups Alive – Church Alive: The Effective Use of Small Groups in the Local Church*, Harper & Row, 1969.

M   Ministry

The best definition of 'ministry' is 'one Christian acting in love to someone else'. The ministry of prayer should be constant. If someone mentions a need it may be helpful to pray for that need immediately, rather than waiting for the 'Time of Prayer'. Talking through a problem or sharing a joy is an important part of ministry. Occasionally the laying on of hands with prayer may be appropriate.

The balance between the different elements of PSALM is important

- Too much prayer and praise, and it becomes a prayer meeting.
- Too much sharing, and it becomes too based on experience.
- Too much action, and there is no centre of prayer and learning.
- Too much learning, and it becomes all head and no heart.
- Too much ministry, and it becomes a counselling group.

Every part of PSALM needs to come from the experiences of the group. If you find one part being squeezed out, think why this is and adjust the balance.

Meals and ministry

To eat or not to eat?

Emmaus leaders are sometimes so keen on the spiritual side of the group that they forget the social. Fellowship comes from:

- feeling you can be open with each other;
- discovering God together;
- praying together;

and enjoying each other's company.

Leaders need to provide the setting in which this can flourish. The normal group meetings do not always make this possible. Hence the need for occasional social opportunities.

Having a meal together can be one way of doing this – but we should not be tied to eating! Other possibilities which have been tried include:

- Going to the cinema or theatre.
- Walking.
- An outing.
- Having a weekend 'retreat'.
- Doing some task together (mowing the churchyard is one example – entertaining a residential home for the elderly is another).

Include in rather than exclude out.

Of particular value in this sort of occasion is the possibility of including friends or family of group members. It is good for them to meet 'those strange people who Dad goes to on a Tuesday evening'. Indeed they might well be members on the next course.

Many of these social possibilities explain themselves but two need underlining:

Meals

The food is important but not so significant as the atmosphere. It is possible to make surroundings so formal that despite excellent food everyone feels ill at ease. Fish and chips out of newspaper or a barbecue may give a more relaxed atmosphere.

Take into account:

1. The social mix of the group. Nobody should be made to feel uncomfortable by the venue or by what happens. We want people to unwind and relax with each other.

2. Sitting down at a table together may well not be possible because of space – it also anchors people so that they can only speak to a few people. A buffet where people can wander may be easier. Barbecues lend themselves to informality.

3. However, if you have a buffet, make sure the food can be eaten with a fork or with fingers.

4. It can share the load of preparing the meal if everyone brings something – organized at the previous session. People feel more at ease if they have contributed, even if it is only a packet of biscuits or something to drink. It also helps to answer the question, 'Who pays?' (The meal where everyone contributes is called different things in different parts of the country – faith supper… fuddle… Jacob's Joint.)

5. Are games appropriate? They can be an excellent way of helping people to mix or can be an interruption in the flow of the party. Have one or two up your sleeve in case things drag, but don't interrupt a party that is going well just because you have prepared a game.

6. Have any members of the group any particular talent: singing, conjuring, playing an instrument, comedy…? If the more reserved members of the group have anything to contribute they should be encouraged. Social gatherings of this kind discover each other's gifts – 'never dreamt old so-and-so could be so funny'; 'what a lovely voice she has'.

7. It is not necessary to have an 'epilogue' as though we have to remind people about God. The social may stand on its own merits and a 'religious slot' can seem intrusive and 'toe-curling'. 'Grace' before the meal would be a reminder of God and the less fortunate people in the world.

How often?

Some groups have a meal almost every time they meet. A lot depends on the sort of people in the group and the time they meet. If those living by themselves have to dash back from work, bolt their supper and then get round to the group, it can be a kindness to provide something to eat – but remember that those with families hardly get to see their partner and children that evening.

Groups which meet in the morning or afternoon may not have the same need to provide food. Indeed parents with young children may see it as a waste of time.

However, most groups find that an occasional 'party' can be a good relaxation for an *Emmaus* group, in which case a whole session can be given over to it.

Special events

The following have been found helpful:

Mid-course meal

During the Nurture course the completion of one group of sessions can be marked by a service (see Nurture course, p.109). Afterwards the congregation can lay on a special meal for those on the course and their families and friends. The opportunity can be taken to explain the course briefly to the guests (and perhaps to invite them to join a new group).

End of course celebration (sometimes called 'Party with a Purpose')

It is particularly appropriate at the end of the Nurture stage to have a party when those who have been on the course have an opportunity to invite their friends and relations and, possibly, say what the course has meant to them. This can be followed by an outline of the course and an invitation to join the next course. This is a form of outreach in which some of the members are the witnesses, and needs careful preparation. Some churches have found this a most fruitful evangelistic opportunity.

Emmaus outreach

At some point in an *Emmaus* Growth group, the group members themselves can put on a party (or other evangelistic event) where they are in charge of the praying, the inviting, the organization and the event itself. This is best if it arises naturally from discussion in the group, which may or may not be while the subject of witness is being explored.

Poverty action

A group can lay on a meal for the homeless or for pensioners. This is best done in conjunction with a church's ongoing social programme.

Going away

An overnight stay or a weekend away can be an excellent way of helping a group to grow closer and for good learning to be done. Some of the questions which need to be answered before embarking on this are:

1. Is there somewhere nearby which can provide comfortable surroundings with good food? Retreat/conference centres are obvious but out-of-season hotels, schools, colleges can often be good value.

2. How much will it cost and how can this be met? If members are to be asked to contribute, will this embarrass or exclude any?

3. If any members have young children how can they be catered for?

4. Is there a subject which lends itself to consecutive teaching and ministry? Teaching and ministry on the person and challenge of Christ and/or the work of the Holy Spirit are possibilities (as suggested in *Growth: Knowing God* – 'Come Holy Spirit') but prayer and many other subjects can also be considered.

    a) At a weekend it is important to vary the educational methods – discussion, role plays, teaching, quiet times for reflection and personal prayer and/or reading, etc. should be considered.

b) It may be appropriate to bring in a speaker from outside – though this alters the dynamics of the group, and not always for the better.

c) The opportunities for worship should be used well. The best seems to be worship which has recognizable connections with what happens in your home church, but is freer, more experimental and relaxed.

d) A time away gives a wonderful opportunity for personal ministry and this needs to be carefully organized and prayed through.

5   Allow plenty of time for relaxation and fun. Many will arrive tired at the end of a working week. A social (on weekends this is traditionally on Saturday evening) can uncover hidden talent. It is probably wise for a weekend away to end with Sunday lunch.

6   If a residential time away is impossible, consider a day away in a different setting with meals provided. Much can be done on a Saturday which runs from, say, 10 a.m. to 8.30 p.m. A weekend can be constructed in this way with members going away on both the Saturday and Sunday but returning home for the night. This can be done at a fraction of the cost of a residential 'retreat'.

Epilogue

A group of ordinary people going along a road… different people going at different speeds:

- Some stop for a while looking confused and then rush ahead again.
- Others plod along purposefully.
- Some go backwards for a time and then start forward again.

Among them walks the Stranger – he seems to be here there and everywhere and manages to talk to everyone. Some of the people have little hats on them labelled 'Leader' – but they are walking along with the rest. They introduce people to the Stranger, but they spend a lot of time talking to him themselves.

Though they do not know it they are all on the way to Emmaus with Cleopas and his companion.

And the leaders have the awesome task of helping people to meet the Stranger.

Some do it more successfully than others:

Let's listen to two people in two different groups. It is the first session of a Nurture group.

Paul's thoughts

They call this a Nurture group – silly name: nurture is all about babies. It's spooky ten of us sitting round a room with the 'leaders' in the big chairs by the fire. There's only one other man. I only came because Jill was so keen on it – but she knows all about church. Those two 'leaders' over there – they couldn't fight their way out of a paper bag – all hot air. I only asked one question but they couldn't answer it – just gave me a fake smile and said we'd think about it later. It's like being back at school: they think I don't know anything. That woman on the other side of the room feels like me: I can tell she is a rebel – you can tell she's read a lot of books and thought a lot. The rest haven't said a word because the leaders have done all the talking – they just say 'Any comments?' and then rush on before you have time to think. Look at them – gabbling on and on and on about things I've never heard of before in a funny sort of jargon. I wonder if the two of them are wound up and this is making them talk a lot.

When I arrived with Jill they hadn't a clue who I was – gave me a bright smile and then talked to Jill about church. The coffee and cakes were all right, I suppose – though I could have used a pint of lager myself.

Deep down I've got lots of questions and I've wondered about God a bit, but this isn't the place to talk about it…

Margaret's thoughts

I'm beginning to relax at last. It's a long time since I came to such a big house but they made me feel at home – asked me to pour out the tea. Darren and Mary are the leaders they seem quite nice and they were interested in me – I think they knew that Alfred had walked out on me last year. So far it's not been over my head and I can read that bit of paper at home where I can take it nice and slow. That Bible scares me – what if they ask me to read a bit – I couldn't, I really couldn't, not in front of all these people.

…and fifteen minutes later…

I said I would come if I never had to say a word. Well, I've surprised myself I asked a question – I had to wind myself up but I got it out – and everybody started talking about it – I felt quite important. They were talking about prayer so I asked if you had to go to church to pray they said that you could pray everywhere which was a relief because I pray when I get into bed.

I think I'm going to like this – they seem a friendly lot of people and some of them seem to have problems of their own. I might even go to church next Sunday – but what do I wear? – and can I take the dog? – and I always go to visit Elsie on a Sunday.

Bibliography on teaching adults

Anton Baumohl, *Making Adult Disciples*, Scripture Union, 1984.

Yvonne Craig, *Learning for Life*, Continuum, 1994.

Mary Howard, *How to Teach Adults*, How to Books, 1996.

Michael Kindred, *Once upon a Group*, 4Mpublications (20 Dover Street, Southwell, Nottinghamshire), 1998.

Alan Rogers, *Teaching Adults*, Open University Press, 2002 (3rd edition).

Jenny Rogers, *Adults Learning*, Open University Press, 2001 (4th edition).

The authors

Stephen Cottrell is the Bishop of Reading. Prior to this he was Canon Pastor at Peterborough Cathedral and also worked for Springboard, the Archbishops' initiative for evangelism. His books include *Catholic Evangelism, Praying Through Life, I Thirst,* the Archbishop of Canterbury's Lent book for 2004, and, with Steven Croft, *Travelling Well: A companion guide to the Christian life.*

Steven Croft is Warden of Cranmer Hall within St John's College, Durham. He was previously Vicar of Ovenden in Halifax for nine years and Mission Consultant in the Diocese of Wakefield. He is author of the handbooks *Growing New Christians* and *Making New Disciples,* and his work has pioneered understanding of the relationship between evangelism and nurture. His recent work includes *Ministry in Three Dimensions: Ordination and Leadership in the Local Church* and *Transforming Communities.*

John Finney is the retired Bishop of Pontefract and former Decade of Evangelism Officer for the Church of England. His research report *Finding Faith Today* has been instrumental in helping the Church understand how people become Christians. He was also involved in the writing of *On the Way – Towards and Integrated Approach to Christian Initiation* for General Synod and is the author of several books on evangelism and renewal.

Felicity Lawson has been Dean of Ministry and Director of Ordinands in the Diocese of Wakefield. Together with John Finney she wrote *Saints Alive!,* a nurture course helping Christians towards a deeper understanding of the life in the Spirit. She has recently returned to parish ministry as Vicar of Gildersome, near Leeds.

Robert Warren was Team Rector of one of the largest and fastest growing churches in England, St Thomas, Crookes. In 1993 he succeeded John Finney as the Church of England's National Officer for Evangelism. In 1998 he became a full-time member of the Springboard team. He is the author of a number of books, including *Building Missionary Congregations,* which points to the task of helping people on the journey of faith as one of the key tasks for the Church in the twenty-first century, and *The Healthy Churches' Handbook.*

Although all five authors are Anglicans, the *Emmaus* material can be used by any denomination and has been produced with this in mind.

Emmaus: The Way of Faith

If you have enjoyed using *Leading an Emmaus Group*, you may be interested in the other *Emmaus: The Way of Faith* material. This resource is aimed at adults and is designed to help churches welcome people into the Christian faith and the life of the Church. It is rooted in an understanding of evangelism, nurture and discipleship that is modelled on the example of Jesus, as portrayed in the story of the Emmaus road.

Emmaus has three stages: **contact, nurture** and **growth**. It begins by encouraging the vision of the local church for evangelism and giving practical advice on how to develop **contact** with those outside the Church. The course material provided includes a 15-week **nurture** course that covers the basics of the Christian life and four **growth** books that offer Christians an opportunity to deepen their understanding of Christian living and discipleship.

Emmaus: The Way of Faith Introduction (2nd edition)
£4.95   978 0 7151 4324 7
Essential background to both the theology and practice of *Emmaus* and includes material on how to run the course in your own church.

Leading an Emmaus Group (2nd edition)
£5.95   978 0 7151 4025 3
Straightforward and direct guide to leading both Nurture and Growth groups. It lays a biblical framework for group leadership, using Jesus as the example and model.

Contact (2nd edition)
£6.95   978 0 7151 4308 7
Explores ways that your church can be involved in evangelism and outreach and make contact with those outside the Church.

Nurture (2nd edition)
£25.50   978 0 7151 4228 8   Includes CD-ROM
A 15-session course covering the basics of Christian life and faith.

Growth: Knowing God (2nd edition)
£22.50   978 0 7151 4032 1
Four short courses for growing Christians: Living the Gospel; Knowing the Father; Knowing Jesus; and Come, Holy Spirit.

Growth: Growing as a Christian (2nd edition)
£22.50   978 0 7151 4014 7   Includes CD-ROM
Five short courses for growing Christians: Growing in Prayer; Growing in the Scriptures; Being Church; Growing in Worship; and Life, Death and Christian Hope.

Growth: Christian Lifestyle (2nd edition)
£22.50   978 0 7151 4006 2   Includes CD-ROM
Four short courses for growing Christians: Living Images; Overcoming Evil; Personal Identity; and Called into Life.

Youth Emmaus (2nd edition)
£25.00   978 0 7151 4364 3   Includes CD-ROM
Aimed specifically at young people aged 11–16, *Youth Emmaus* tackles the basics of the Christian faith. Ideal for teenage confirmation candidates.

Youth Emmaus 2
£22.00   978 0 7151 4048 2   Includes CD-ROM
A discipleship course teaching young people aged 11-16 how to integrate their faith into life and grow as worshippers and disciples.

Emmaus Bible Resources – Ideal for small groups!
Finding a middle ground between daily Bible notes and weighty commentaries, the series adopts the *Emmaus* approach of combining sound theology and good educational practice with a commitment to equip the whole Church for mission.

Each book contains leader's guidelines, short prayers or meditations, a commentary, discussion questions and practical 'follow-on' activities.

The Lord is Risen!
Luke 24
Steven Croft   £7.95   978 0 7151 4323 0
The Lord is Risen! takes us on a journey through Luke that strengthens, challenges, deepens and renews our Christian discipleship. An ideal 'Easter' book.

Missionary Journeys, Missionary Church
Acts 13-20
Steven Croft   £9.99   978 0 7151 4346 9
Throughout Christian history, men and women have returned to the book of Acts to find their faith and ministry renewed and rekindled.

A Rebellious Prophet
Jonah
Joy Tetley   £7.95   978 0 7151 4986 7

As Christians, we are not all called to be prophets. But we are all called to respond to God's prompting. This study of the book of Jonah challenges us to do just that.

Christ our Life
Colossians
David Day   £9.99   978 0 7151 4352 0

Colossians was written to a church set in a culture dominated by powerful forces and alternative spiritualities. David Day's perceptive book encourages us to consider how to give Christ his rightful place in every area of our lives, both personal and corporate.

Related titles

How to Live
A Guide for the Christian Journey
Stephen Cottrell and Steven Croft
£9.99   978 0 7151 4240 0

Provides instruction for important areas in Christian life such as prayer, reading the Bible, worship and relating faith to daily life. Ideal for adult Christians who are beginning the journey of faith.

How to Pray
Alone, with Others At Any Time In Any Place
Stephen Cottrell
£8.99   978 0 7151 4222 6

This is a book for novices, not experts. *How to Pray* explores ways to start, renew and expand our prayer life, whether by ourselves or with others. It helps us discover how natural prayer can be, even when we least feel like it.